Our Covenant With GOD

KENNETH
COPELAND
PUBLICATIONS

All scripture is from the *King James Version* of the Bible.

Our Covenant With God

ISBN-10 1-57562-242-4   30-0008
ISBN-13 978-1-57562-242-2

15 14 13 12 11 10   16 15 14 13 12 11

© 1976 Kenneth Copeland

Kenneth Copeland Publications
Fort Worth, TX 76192-0001

For more information about Kenneth Copeland Ministries,
call 800-600-7395 or visit www.kcm.org.

Contents

Introduction

Introduction

One of the most embarrassing situations for any businessman is to find out he has lost vast sums of money needlessly or to learn of assets he could have been enjoying for years simply because he did not know the fullness of the contracts he had entered into.

I remember the story of a poor man who scrimped and saved every cent until he could buy a ticket on a great ship to come to America. He only had enough money left to buy some cheese and a little bread to eat on the trip. He would gaze longingly into the dining rooms and watch the people eat the beautiful food and enjoy themselves. On the morning of their New York arrival, one of the ship's officers asked the man if they had offended him in any way since he had not eaten his meals with them. "Oh, no!" the man replied. "I only had enough money to pay for my ticket. I didn't have enough to eat in the dining rooms." The officer looked at the man almost in disbelief and said, "Sir, I'm so sorry. Your meals were included in your fare."

So many Christian people are living on bread and cheese when God's best is theirs all the time. They don't know the terms of their contract, their covenant—the New Testament. I believe this book will help you find out what belongs to you in your covenant with Jesus.

1
Abraham's Covenant

In the beginning God created the heavens and the earth. Genesis 1:26-27 says:

And God said, Let us make man in our image, after our likeness: and let them have dominion over the fish of the sea, and over the fowl of the air, and over the cattle, and over all the earth, and over every creeping thing that creepeth upon the earth. So God created man in his own image, in the image of God created he him; male and female created he them.

From the dust of the earth, God formed a man, named him Adam, and placed him in the midst of the Garden of Eden. This man Adam was given the awesome authority of lordship over God's creation on earth. God gave him dominion over every living thing on the face of this earth. He was to subdue the earth and replenish it. He was given the right to be the father of God's family. He was to sire the human race. What a privilege!

God set a law into motion at Creation which I call *the law of genesis*—or the law of beginnings. According to this law, every living thing was created by God to produce after its own kind. Man was no exception. God is a Spirit, and Adam was created in God's own image and likeness—a spirit being. They walked in close fellowship and communion together, and Adam's descendants were to live in harmony with God, their spiritual Father. But something happened in the Garden that caused a great and terrible change to occur. Satan approached Adam's wife Eve and deceived her into disobeying God's command. Then Adam willfully followed her in this rebellion.

According to the law of genesis, man takes on the nature of his spiritual father or lord. God was Adam's spiritual father. But when Adam disobeyed God and bowed his knee to Satan, he changed spiritual fathers. Satan became the illegitimate stepfather of mankind. Adam committed high treason. At that point, all the dominion and authority God had given him was handed over to Satan. Suddenly, God was on the outside looking in.

Until this time, Satan did not have any authority on earth. All his authority had been taken away when he led the rebellion against God in heaven (Isaiah 14:12). He came into the picture absolutely void of authority. But by deceiving the woman, he manipulated man's authority into his own hands and became the god of this world (2 Corinthians 4:4). In Luke 4:3-7, when Satan tempted Jesus in the wilderness, he took Jesus up on a high mountain and showed Him all the kingdoms of the earth. He said, "All this power will I give thee, and the glory of them: for that is delivered unto me: and to whomsoever I will I give it. If thou therefore will worship me, all shalt be thine" (Luke 4:6-7).

Some people think this was just one of Satan's lies. But if it had been

a lie, it would not have been a temptation and the Bible says that Jesus was
sorely tempted. This was *real* temptation, brother! Satan had it to give.
Jesus was tempted, but He used the
weapon for which there is no defense.
He said, "It is written..." and Satan had
to flee from Him!

After the Fall of Adam, God was
in a peculiar position. He had given
Adam unquestionable authority over
the earth. But when Adam committed
high treason against God and bowed
his knee to Satan, spiritual death—the
nature of Satan—was lodged in his
heart. Actually, Adam was the first
person ever to be born again. He was
born from spiritual life to spiritual
death. God had said, "But of the tree of
the knowledge of good and evil, thou
shalt not eat of it: for in the day that
thou eatest thereof thou shalt surely
die" (Genesis 2:17).

God said that Adam would die the
very day he ate the forbidden fruit, yet
he lived several hundred years longer. God was not referring to physical
death. He meant that Adam would die

spiritually—that he would take on the nature of Satan, which is spiritual death.

This process is reversed when you make Jesus the Lord of your life. You are born from death into life. The law of spiritual lordship is our way back into the hands of God. You take on a new Lord and receive the nature of your new Lord which is eternal life (John 3:16). This is why Jesus went to the cross. First John 3:8 says, "For this purpose the Son of God was manifested, that he might destroy the works of the devil." Jesus turned to the most religious men of His day and said, "Ye are of your father the devil" (John 8:44). By going to the cross as the sinless Son of God, Jesus took away the dominion Satan had over mankind. First Corinthians 2:8 states that had the princes of this world known, they would never have crucified the Lord of glory. This was a trap that the Father and Jesus had set for Satan. He walked into it, and it cost him his lordship over the earth.

After Adam's Fall in the Garden, God needed an avenue back into the earth. He needed some way to break the union between Satan and mankind. Since man was the key figure in the Fall, man had to be the key figure in the redemption, so God approached a man named Abram. He re-enacted with Abram what Satan had done with Adam, except that God did not sneak in and use deception, as Satan had. God offered Abram a proposition and Abram bought it.

Let's look at Genesis 17:1-5 for a moment and examine this agreement God made with Abram:

And when Abram was ninety years old and nine, the Lord appeared to Abram, and said unto him, I am the Almighty God; walk before me, and be thou perfect. And I will make my covenant between me and thee, and will multiply thee exceedingly. And Abram fell on his face: and God talked with him, saying, As for me, behold, my covenant is with thee, and thou shalt be a father of many nations. Neither shall thy name any more be called Abram, but thy name shall be Abraham; for a father of many nations have I made thee.

Notice particularly that God said, "As for me...." You see, Abram did not have to accept God's deal. He was not being forced to do anything—it was his own free choice. God laid out His proposition and Abram accepted it. It gave God access to the earth and gave man access to God. At this time man had no real knowledge of God's nature. People only knew what their fathers had passed down to them. After Adam died and several generations passed, no one really knew much about God anymore.

You need to understand the authority that was placed in the covenant. This was an absolute agreement between God and Abram, sealed on both sides. God sealed His side of the agreement by swearing by Himself (Genesis 22:16). In other words, there *is* no higher state that God can swear by, so He swore by Himself. Technically, if He ever broke the covenant, He would have to destroy Himself.

The Hebrew word *covenant* means "to cut where blood flows." This is the strongest agreement in any language. A covenant is a contract, or agreement, made between two parties and sealed by the shedding of their blood. Once this is done, the covenant can never be broken. Every heathen tribe on the face of the earth has a blood covenant. The blood covenant between God and man was marked and sealed in man's flesh through circumcision (Genesis 17:10-14). In other words, circumcision was "the cut of the covenant."

From that time forward, Abram was a covenant man with God. God even changed his name to Abraham. In Genesis 18:17-33 we find God consulting with His covenant man about the destruction of Sodom and Gomorrah. Can you see the strength of this covenant? It was powerful!

The book of Exodus provides more insight into the strength of the covenant through what took place among the Israelites in Egypt and then during their wanderings in the wilderness. Exodus 2:23-25 says, "And the children of Israel sighed by reason of the bondage, and they cried, and their cry came up unto God by reason of the bondage. And God heard their groaning, and God remembered his covenant with Abraham, with Isaac, and with Jacob. And God looked upon the children of Israel, and God had respect unto them."

God remembered His covenant with Abraham and in behalf of that covenant found a man named Moses herding sheep on the backside of the desert. God called him to lead the Israelites out of Egypt.

After the Israelites were set free and journeyed into the wilderness, we find another situation so critical that Moses went on his face before God for forty days without food or water. This is the only fast in the entire Bible where a man goes without drink. It had to be a supernatural existence because Moses would have died without liquid. But he just refused to let go of God. Exodus 32:9-10, "And the Lord said unto Moses, I have seen this people, and, behold, it is a stiffnecked people: Now therefore let me alone, that my wrath may wax hot against them, and that I may consume them: and I will make of thee a great nation." God wanted to destroy Israel and start a new race with Moses as He had with Noah after the Flood. In verses 11-14 it says:

Moses besought the Lord his God, and said, Lord, why doth thy wrath wax hot against thy people, which thou hast brought forth out of the land of Egypt with great power, and with a mighty hand?...Turn from thy fierce wrath, and repent of this evil against thy people. Remember Abraham, Isaac, and Israel, thy servants, to whom thou swarest by thine own self, and saidst unto them, I will multiply your seed as the stars of heaven, and all this land that I have spoken of will I give unto your seed, and they shall inherit it for ever. And the Lord repented of the evil which he thought to do unto his people.

God repented! Why? Because of the covenant He had made with Abraham so many years before.

2
The Blessing of Abraham

God promised to care for Abraham and his descendants in every way—spiritually, physically, financially, socially. In Genesis 17:7 God said to Abraham, "And I will establish my covenant between me and thee...to be a God unto thee, and to thy seed after thee." The Hebrew name for Almighty God is *El Shaddai. El* means "supreme;" *Shaddai* means "the breasty one." In other words, God was promising to be their father, their mother, their nurse—the supreme provider of everything they would need in life. He spoke the words of the covenant and swore by Himself to keep it. This was an iron-clad agreement.

The people of Israel badly trampled the covenant at Mount Sinai, but through Moses' intervention, God forgave them. At this point, God handed down the Law and instituted the Levitical priesthood to help repair the damage that had been done. God was sworn to their destruction for breaking the

covenant, but instead He allowed sacrificial offerings to cover their sins. The
Levitical priesthood was brought into
existence for one purpose: to bridge the
gap between God and mankind.

Hebrews 9:22 states that "without
shedding of blood is no remission
(of sin)." There had to be a mediator
between God and Israel because of the
existence of the blood covenant. The
first mediator was the Levitical priesthood. The last mediator was Jesus—
our High Priest who ever liveth to
make intercession for us (1 Timothy
2:5; Hebrews 7:25).

In Deuteronomy 28:1-14, Moses
recorded God's law and the articles of
the covenant, listing the blessings of
God promised to those who will put
His Word first place in their lives.

And it shall come to pass, if thou
shalt hearken diligently unto the
voice of the Lord thy God, to observe
and to do all his commandments
which I command thee this day,
that the Lord thy God will set thee
on high above all the nations of the

earth: And all these blessings shall come on thee, and overtake thee, if thou shalt hearken unto the voice of the Lord thy God. Blessed shalt thou be in the city, and blessed shalt thou be in the field. Blessed shall be the fruit of thy body, and the fruit of thy ground, and the fruit of thy cattle, the increase of thy kine, and the flocks of thy sheep. Blessed shall be thy basket and thy store. Blessed shalt thou be when thou comest in, and blessed shalt thou be when thou goest out. The Lord shall cause thine enemies that rise up against thee to be smitten before thy face: they shall come out against thee one way, and flee before thee seven ways. The Lord shall command the blessing upon thee in thy storehouses, and in all that thou settest thine hand unto; and he shall bless thee in the land which the Lord thy God giveth thee. The Lord shall establish thee an holy people unto himself, as he hath sworn unto thee, if thou shalt keep the commandments of the Lord thy God, and walk in his ways. And all the people of the earth shall see that thou art called by the name of the Lord; and they shall be afraid of thee. And the Lord shall make thee plenteous in goods, in the fruit of thy body, and in the fruit of thy cattle, and in the fruit of thy ground, in the land which the Lord sware unto thy fathers to give thee. The Lord shall open unto thee his good treasure, the heaven to give the rain unto thy land in his season, and to bless all the work of thine hand: and thou shalt lend unto many nations, and thou shalt not borrow. And the Lord shall make thee the head, and not the tail; and thou shalt be above only, and thou shalt not be beneath; if that thou hearken unto the commandments of the Lord thy God, which I command thee this day, to observe and to do them: And thou shalt not go aside from any of the words which I command thee this day, to the right hand, or to the left, to go after other gods to serve them.

Praise the Lord! This is the blessing of Abraham. I want you to notice that it covers every area of life—spiritual, physical, mental, financial, social and political.

Mighty armies have come against the people of Israel and failed miserably. As long as the Israelites were walking under the covenant of God, as long as they were doing what God said to do in His Word, they were not harmed. His agreement with them said, "If an enemy comes out at you one way, I will cause him to flee seven ways."

Some people have said, "Yes, Brother Copeland, but that's what God promised to do for the Jews." No, this promise was given to Abraham and to *all* his descendants. That means it belongs to you through faith in Jesus Christ, as much as it does to the Israelites. Galatians 3:29 says, "And if ye be Christ's, then are ye Abraham's seed, and heirs according to the promise."

As a born-again child of God you are now Abraham's seed. These blessings belong to you, too.

3
The Curse of the Law

When a man under the Abrahamic Covenant refused to obey the law that would bring the blessing, there was only one alternative—the curse. When a man steps out from under the covenant with God, he automatically steps back over into the hands of Satan. The curse was already in the earth from the time that Adam bowed his knee to Satan in the Garden. It was only God's covenant that protected the people from being completely destroyed by Satan. Abraham had plenty of problems before God approached him. What he did not have was a way out of the problems. There is no area where a man can stand in the middle between the blessings of God and the problems of the world. If he doesn't have the blessings of God, he has the problems of the world. There's no in-between.

When God made His covenant with Abraham, He didn't do away with the curse. He just offered Abraham a way to live free from its effect by providing an umbrella of protection. He said, "If you will walk perfect and upright before Me, I'll protect you." Thus Abraham and his descendants would be protected from the curse already in the world. However, when they stepped from beneath the protection of God's Word, Satan was waiting to come against them.

Let's look at the curse beginning in Deuteronomy 28:15-19:

> But it shall come to pass, if thou wilt not hearken unto the voice of the Lord thy God, to observe to do all his commandments and his statutes which I command thee this day; that all these curses shall come upon thee, and overtake thee: Cursed shalt thou be in the city, and cursed shalt thou be in the field. Cursed shall be thy basket and thy store. Cursed shall be the fruit of thy body, and the fruit of thy land, the increase of thy kine, and of the flocks of thy sheep. Cursed shalt thou be when

thou comest in, and cursed shalt thou be when thou goest out.

The next several verses refer to many different plagues and diseases that are part of this curse. Verse 29 mentions poverty, "And thou shalt not prosper in thy ways: and thou shalt be only oppressed and spoiled evermore, and no man shall save thee." It goes on to list marital difficulties, cattle destruction, sickness in the legs and knees, sores that cannot be healed, crop destruction.

Verse 44 refers to being in debt, "He (the stranger) shall lend to thee, and thou shalt not lend to him: he shall be the head, and thou shalt be the tail."

Verse 61 says, "Also every sickness, and every plague, which is not written in the book of this law, them will the Lord bring upon thee, until thou be destroyed." So, *all* sickness and *all* disease—even those not mentioned here—come under the curse.

4
Our Redemption

"Christ hath redeemed us from the curse of the law, being made a curse for us: for it is written, Cursed is every one that hangeth on a tree: That the blessing of Abraham might come on the Gentiles through Jesus Christ; that we might receive the promise of the Spirit through faith" (Galations 3:13-14).

Jesus of Nazareth was a product of the Abrahamic Covenant. He was an Israelite circumcised the eighth day. As we have read from Genesis 17:1, God commanded that Abraham walk perfect and upright before Him; but it was not until Jesus that this command was fulfilled. Jesus walked perfect before God under the articles of the covenant, and God backed His ministry 100 percent. He used the covenant to control the laws of nature. He spoke the words that broke the bonds of death and brought Lazarus forth from the grave. God was bound by His own words to do what Jesus said. The Bible tells us in Hebrews 4:15 that Jesus was "in all points tempted like as we are, yet without sin." He faced as much temptation to sin as any man on earth, yet He withstood it all and continued to walk perfect before God.

According to Levitical law, the high priest was to take an unblemished lamb and offer it as a sacrifice for sin. Jesus of Nazareth, the unblemished Lamb of God, served as the final sacrifice for sin under the Abrahamic Covenant. The High Priest offered up the spotless Son of God on the altar of the cross for the sins of mankind. The blood of Jesus was poured out in behalf of the covenant He upheld. He was our substitute—bearing our sins, diseases, poverty and spiritual death.

Remember what was listed under the curse in Deuteronomy 28? Poverty of every kind, political failure, drought, war—every calamity known to mankind. Jesus has redeemed us from all of it. As we saw in Deuteronomy 28:61, *all* sickness and *all* disease, even those not mentioned there, come under the curse. Therefore, we are redeemed from all sickness and all disease. You need to fight the temptation to be sick just as you would fight the temptation to lie or steal. Satan will tempt you with sickness, but you don't have to give in. You can resist him with the Word of God like Jesus did!

Jesus fulfilled the terms of the old covenant and brought a new covenant into being—a better covenant based on better promises. He died and paid the price to finish that old Abrahamic Covenant. He satisfied it completely and was resurrected from the dead a new man—a new covenant man untouchable by sin, untouchable by death. Now He is seated at the right hand of God to carry out this new covenant.

The new covenant is between Almighty God and Jesus Christ, an immortal man incapable of failure. God will not fail, Jesus will not fail. Therefore, the covenant between them will not fail! Jesus was capable of failure when He walked the shores of Galilee. He had to stand the test Adam failed, and He stood it without failure.

As the Son of God, Jesus accepted the penalty of death for sin. He was taken illegally by Satan into the bowels of the earth. But God proclaimed, "It is enough!" and Jesus came forth out of hell triumphant in the power of God! The courts of eternal justice were satisfied. Sin was completely remitted—wiped away. God took man's place and suffered the penalty for breaking the covenant. Man once again has legal right to enter the Father's presence in the holy of holies (Hebrews 4:14-16).

The cut of the old covenant was the shedding of man's blood through circumcision. The cut of the new covenant was the shedding of God's blood on the cross by Jesus, the Lamb of God—the sacrificial lamb that took away the sins of the world (John 1:29). There is no curse under the new covenant because Jesus became the curse for us! Praise God!

5
The Seed of Abraham

We have read from Galatians 3:13-14 that Jesus Christ has redeemed us from the curse of the law so that we might receive the blessing of Abraham and the promise of the Spirit. Let's take this a little bit further and discuss it in more depth.

In Galatians 3:16 we read, "Now to Abraham and his seed were the promises made. He saith not, And to seeds, as of many; but as of one, And to thy seed, which is Christ." God's promise was made through Abraham, but it was actually meant for one person, Jesus Christ. We have seen from the book of Genesis that God approached Abram with His proposition for a covenant between them. God's purpose was to provide an avenue back into the earth—to open the way for Jesus to come forth.

In his lifetime, Abraham operated only basic parts of God's covenant. In the following years, God revealed more of His Word to the prophets. These

Old Testament prophets handled the
Word and operated under the covenant, but the promise was made to
Abraham's seed—Jesus Christ. They
used the covenant as best they could,
but it was too difficult for them to
follow completely. They were just not
strong enough spiritually to handle it,
but Jesus was! *The promise was made to
one seed, which is Christ.*

Throughout the Old Testament,
God promised to care for His people
in every way—spirit, soul and body.
He said, "I will protect you from your
enemies. If they come against you one
way, they will flee seven ways. I will
be your God and you will be My people." In Isaiah 58:9, God said, "Then
shalt thou call, and the Lord shall answer...." In the Hebrew language this
literally means, "You call and the Lord
will answer, even before you finish the
sentence." God made these promises,
and they were perfectly fulfilled in the
ministry of Jesus. When Jesus spoke,
God moved! He said, "Peace, be still!"
and the hand of God fell on that
storm so strongly that it had to cease!

Jesus said, "Lazarus, come forth!" and Lazarus had no choice but to come forth from the grave!

We need to realize why these things took place in Jesus' earthly ministry. It was not because He was the spotless Son of God. Jesus did not minister as the Son of God. He could have. He was God manifest in the flesh. The important thing to us is that He didn't. Jesus ministered on earth as a prophet under the Abrahamic Covenant. He ministered the principles in the Word of God to Israel in faith and in the love of God. Some people have the idea that Jesus introduced healing to the world, but healing was a provision of the covenant from the beginning. Jesus did not use one tool in His earthly ministry that was not available to every Israelite through their covenant with God. He didn't use His *Sonship* as a weapon against Satan. He used the Word of God and said, "It is written...." His weapons were the written Word of God, faith in His Father, and the gifts of the Holy Spirit. He said, "The Father that dwelleth in me, he doeth the works" (John 14:10).

Everything Jesus used in His earthly ministry is available to the believer today. The only thing Jesus did that no other person on earth could ever do was to die on the cross as the Son of God and pay the price for sin. God did not answer Jesus' prayers simply because He was His Son. He answered Jesus' prayers because of the covenant (the promise), that Jesus was operating under—the covenant that God had allowed Abraham to handle so many years before.

In the light of this truth, let's read again from Galatians 3:16-19:

> Now to Abraham and his seed were the promises made. He saith not, And to seeds, as of many; but as of one, And to thy seed, which is Christ. And this I say, that the covenant, that was confirmed before of God in Christ, the law, which was four hundred and thirty years after, cannot disannul, that it should make the promise of none effect. For if the inheritance be of the law, it is no more of promise: but God gave it

to Abraham by promise. Wherefore then serveth the law? It was added because of transgressions, till the seed should come to whom the promise was made.

You see, the law was brought in to protect the promise. Then when Jesus came forth, the promise was in force.

Once God's Word has been loosed in the earth, there is nothing Satan can do about it. Isaiah 55:11 says, "So shall my word be that goeth forth out of my mouth: it shall not return unto me void, but it shall accomplish that which I please, and it shall prosper in the thing whereto I sent it." God's Word *will* come to pass. There is no way Satan can stop it! When you received salvation, when you made the decision and acted on it, no devil in hell was powerful enough to stop the new birth from taking place in your life.

Satan is helpless before the Name of Jesus because the power of the curse has been broken. He will walk all over you if you allow him to, but his actual power has been removed. The power of sin has been broken. Satan cannot dominate you once you recognize the power of the Word of God and allow that power to operate in your life.

In the old covenant, we can see that the power of sin was very much in force. Satan took the authority that Adam had given him and perverted it, using fear and death against men instead of the life and faith they had in God. The power of sin was operating throughout the Old Testament. A man could make the decision to live in line with God's Word, but sin would still plague him night and day. For instance, Noah performed the greatest act of faith known to man and then got roaring drunk! This is why the decisions of the Old Testament saints spoken of in Hebrews 11 were such outstanding feats of faith. The power of sin was still inside them and spiritual death was lodged in their hearts. Then Jesus came to earth. He bore the penalty of spiritual death, broke its power, and was raised from the dead, triumphant over Satan and his kingdom. When you made Jesus your Lord, the power of eternal life enveloped your spirit and a new man was born inside you: "Therefore if any man be in Christ, he is a new creature: old things are passed away; behold, all things are become new. And all things are of God" (2 Corinthians 5:17-18). This is the new covenant!

Wherefore then serveth the law? It was added because of transgressions, till the seed should come to whom the promise was made; and it was ordained by angels in the hand of a mediator. Now a mediator is not a mediator of one, but God is one. Is the law then against the promises of God? God forbid: for if there had been a law given which could have given life, verily righteousness should have been by the law. But the scripture hath concluded all under sin, that the promise by faith of Jesus Christ might be given to them that believe. But before faith came, we were kept under the law, shut up unto the faith which should afterwards be revealed. Wherefore the law was our schoolmaster to bring us unto Christ, that we might be justified by faith. But after that faith is come, we are no longer under a schoolmaster. For ye are all the children of God by faith in Christ Jesus. For as many of you as have been baptized into Christ have put on Christ. There is neither Jew nor Greek, there is neither bond nor free, there is neither male nor female: for ye are all one in Christ Jesus. *And if ye be Christ's, then are ye Abraham's seed,* and heirs according to the promise (Galatians 3:19-29).

If Jesus Christ is the Lord of your life, then *you* are Abraham's seed. Notice the word seed in verse 29 is singular as it was in verse 16, when it was referring to Jesus. The promise is to you and will work in Jesus' Name every bit as well as it did for Jesus in Galilee. You have put on Christ. You are one with Him. Jesus has passed the promise to you as His joint heir! You have the right to function exactly the same way Jesus functioned in the earth by using His Name. It is *your* promise. He has given it to you.

With this understanding, let's look once again at Galatians 3:13-14. "Christ hath redeemed us from the curse of the law...that the blessing of Abraham might come on the Gentiles through Jesus Christ; that we might receive the promise of the Spirit through faith." We have always read this thinking that "the promise of the Spirit" referred to receiving the promised Holy Spirit, but there is more to it. The Holy Spirit is a part of the promise, but this verse actually means that through faith we might receive the promise that the Spirit made to Jesus. It is referring to the entire promise of God given through Abraham.

This promise of God should be so real to you as an individual believer that you will receive it and act upon it the same way Jesus did! However, you must realize that you have to work it according to the Word of God, not according to how you think or feel. The natural mind does not consider prayer answered until the answer can be seen. But prayer is answered the moment you receive the answer by faith from the authority of God's Word. Quit dealing with the problem and begin to deal with the answer from the Word of God. Start confessing the answer before you can see the manifestation. This is what Jesus did! He spoke the end result. Romans 4:17 says that God speaks of things that are not as though they were. We should do the same thing!

The promise God gave to Jesus has now been given to the believer. We are to receive the blessing of Abraham written in Deuteronomy 28. As the seed of Abraham, I intend to receive everything that is mine by Christ Jesus as a glory to God. God's Word tells us that we have a right to pray and expect God to answer, not because of what we have done but because of what Jesus has done for us! God said, "If ye be willing and obedient, ye shall eat the good of the land" (Isaiah 1:19). Obedient to what? The Word of God, the new covenant of God. The old covenant was fulfilled by Jesus on the cross. He walked perfect and upright before God, then took the penalty for breaking the covenant. He went to hell and paid the price for our sin. But because He was sinless, because He had not broken the covenant, hell could not hold Him! He whipped Satan and took the keys of death and hell! (Revelation 1:18).

You can expect God to move because of His Word, because of His promise to Abraham's seed. Find out what the covenant says. Put the Word first place in your life. Matthew 8:17 says, "Himself took our infirmities, and bare our sicknesses." That is God speaking directly to you, the believer. Christ has redeemed *you* from the curse of the law so that the blessing of Abraham will come on *you* through Jesus Christ, that *you* might receive the promise of the Spirit through faith. The blessings of God belong to every born-again believer. All you have to do is stand on God's Word and allow these blessings to manifest themselves in your life.

Deuteronomy 28:7-8 says, "The Lord shall cause thine enemies that rise up against thee to be smitten before thy face: they shall come out against thee one way, and flee before thee seven ways. The Lord shall command the blessing upon thee in thy storehouses...." In Ephesians 1:3, the Apostle Paul wrote that God has "blessed us with all spiritual blessings in heavenly places in Christ." When I first realized this, I thought, *Lord, I've been trying to get You to bless me when You have already commanded the blessings upon me through Jesus Christ.*

As a believer, you have a right to make commands in the Name of Jesus. Each time you stand on the Word, you are commanding God to a certain extent because it is His Word. In Isaiah 45:11, the Lord says: "Ask me of things to come concerning my sons, and concerning the work of my hands *command* ye me."

Whenever an honest man gives you his word, he is bound by it. It is not necessary to order him around because a truly honest man will back his word. When you stand on what he has said, he is "commanded" to do it. In the same way, you put a command on God through His Word. He said, "Put me in remembrance" (Isaiah 43:26). Sometimes I just hold the Bible up to God like a mirror and say, "Father, this is Your Word and I am standing on it. You have said that no weapon formed against me will prosper, so in the Name of Jesus I expect it to be according to Your Word." This places a command on God. Now I don't say, "Look here, God, You have to do this because I said so!" No, that's ridiculous! I simply go before Him in the Name of Jesus and remind Him of His Word.

6
The Daughter of Abraham

Let's look at Luke 13:10-12: "And he was teaching in one of the synagogues on the sabbath. And, behold, there was a woman which had a spirit of infirmity eighteen years, and was bowed together, and could in no wise lift up herself. And when Jesus saw her, he called her to him, and said unto her, Woman, thou art loosed from thine infirmity."

Notice that Jesus did not say, "I am going to loose you" or "Be loosed." He said, "Woman, thou art loosed." Jesus did not waste words; He used them. Words had an extremely high priority in His ministry. "And he laid his hands on her: and immediately she was made straight, and glorified God."

When the ruler of the synagogue questioned Him about healing on the Sabbath day, Jesus said, "And ought not this woman, being a daughter of Abraham, whom Satan hath bound, lo, these eighteen years, be loosed from this bond on the sabbath day?"

(verse 16). That woman was a daughter of Abraham, and therefore had a right to be loosed from that infirmity. You see, she had lived with her infirmity for eighteen years because she didn't know the blessing of Abraham—the blessing that would set her free!

This same ignorance of God's covenant caused Israel to live in bondage for 400 years.

The Word of God was just as valid and real when they went into bondage as it was the day they were set free. The only problem was, they didn't know it. God had to call Moses and explain the covenant to him so that he could lead them out of Egypt. Moses went before Pharaoh in behalf of that covenant and led the Israelites out of bondage. It was the same God, and His Word was just as true 400 years before, but the people had lost sight of it.

Jesus did not pray for that daughter of Abraham. He told her that she was loosed, and then He laid hands on her.

In the Great Commission (Mark 16:15-18), Jesus did not say, "These signs shall follow those that believe...

they shall pray for the sick and they shall recover." Jesus did not mention praying for the sick. He said, "Lay hands on the sick, and they shall recover." There is nothing wrong with praying for the sick, but many times we have our minds so rigid that we miss the reality of the words. He said, "Go ye into all the world, and preach the gospel to every creature." Jesus was saying that the gospel would do the job. When we preach the gospel—the good news, the Word of God—then we can expect the sick to be healed when we lay hands on them. First, we must preach the truth—"that God was in Christ, reconciling the world unto himself, not imputing their trespasses unto them." And that He who knew no sin was made to be sin for us "that we might be made the righteousness of God in him" (2 Corinthians 5:19-21). Preach the truth...the signs will follow!

What is a pair of crippled legs that they would not obey the voice of the righteousness of God? What are blind eyes that they would refuse to see after Jesus said in Luke 4:18, "The Spirit of

the Lord is upon me...to preach...
recovering of sight to the blind"? God
is the Creator. He is the Father. Satan
has no right to run roughshod over
God's children.

"Ought not this woman be loosed,
seeing she is a daughter of Abraham?"

You can apply this to yourself
because "if ye be Christ's, then are ye
Abraham's seed, and heirs according to
the promise." Ought not this man be
loosed from financial bondage, seeing
he is the seed of Abraham? Ought not
this woman be loosed from arthritis,
seeing she is a seed of Abraham?

Jesus spoke the words, "Woman,
thou art loosed from thine infirmity."
Then in honor of the Word of God, He
laid His hands on her. The power it
took to enforce God's Word came into
action and immediately the woman
was set free! Praise the Lord!

I have used this fact of being redeemed from the curse many, many
times. When Satan would come at me
with some problem, I would open my
Bible to Galatians 3:13-14 and say,
"Praise God! I've been redeemed from

that. Satan, you are not going to put that on me. I'll not stand for it!"

When a person lives out from under the curse and is walking uprightly before God, he has the power of God in his corner. He has the power of the Spirit Himself backing him. The Word of God states very clearly in Hebrews 7:22 that Jesus is the surety, or the guarantee, of this new covenant. Jesus Christ of Nazareth will have to fail before the covenant can fail, and in Him there is no failure. Why? Because Jesus is love and love never fails.

Go to the Word. That is what it is for. That is why it was written. It is a copy of your contract—your covenant—with God. It sets out the things God promised Jesus that He would do. Hebrews 1 speaks of Jesus' inauguration as Lord of the universe. It says that He is upholding all things by the Word of His power. If you want to be upheld, get on the Word.

Once you make Jesus Lord over your life, you become a covenant man under the new covenant. Remember God said, "As for Me, these things are so." He said, "As for Me, you are healed. As for Me, you are redeemed from the curse of the law. As for Me, the blessing of Abraham is upon you." The only reason these blessings are not operating in your life is because you have not stood up and said, "Well, as for me, it is so, too!"

Make this confession from your heart before God.

"Father, in the Name of Jesus, I believe in my heart that Jesus has been raised from the dead. I make Him Lord of my life now with the confession of my mouth. I am His and He is mine! Jesus has redeemed me from the curse of the law. Sickness will have to depart. Disease will have to depart. Poverty will no longer be in my house, for I am redeemed from the curse of poverty. I am a believer and not a doubter. I have the Name of Jesus and the power of the Holy Spirit. Thank God, darkness is over. The storms of life will no longer be victorious over me. Jesus is my intercessor. The Spirit of God strengthens me. You, God, are my very own Father. I praise Your Name!"

Prayer for Salvation and Baptism in the Holy Spirit

Heavenly Father, I come to You in the Name of Jesus. Your Word says, "Whosoever shall call on the name of the Lord shall be saved" (Acts 2:21). I am calling on You. I pray and ask Jesus to come into my heart and be Lord over my life according to Romans 10:9-10: "If thou shalt confess with thy mouth the Lord Jesus, and shalt believe in thine heart that God hath raised him from the dead, thou shalt be saved. For with the heart man believeth unto righteousness; and with the mouth confession is made unto salvation." I do that now. I confess that Jesus is Lord, and I believe in my heart that God raised Him from the dead.

I am now reborn! I am a Christian—a child of Almighty God! I am saved! You also said in Your Word, "If ye then, being evil, know how to give good gifts unto your children: HOW MUCH MORE shall your heavenly Father give the Holy Spirit to them that ask him?" (Luke 11:13). I'm also asking You to fill me with the Holy Spirit. Holy Spirit, rise up within me as I praise God. I fully expect to speak with other tongues as You give me the utterance (Acts 2:4). In Jesus' Name. Amen!

Begin to praise God for filling you with the Holy Spirit. Speak those words and syllables you receive—not in your own language, but the language given to you by the Holy Spirit. You have to use your own voice. God will not force you to speak. Don't be concerned with how it sounds. It is a heavenly language!

Continue with the blessing God has given you and pray in the spirit every day.

You are a born-again, Spirit-filled believer. You'll never be the same!

Find a good church that boldly preaches God's Word and obeys it. Become part of a church family who will love and care for you as you love and care for them.

We need to be connected to each other. It increases our strength in God. It's God's plan for us.

Make it a habit to watch the *Believer's Voice of Victory* television broadcast and become a doer of the Word, who is blessed in his doing (James 1:22-25).

About the Author

Kenneth Copeland is co-founder and president of Kenneth Copeland Ministries in Fort Worth, Texas, and best-selling author of books that include *How to Discipline Your Flesh* and *Honor— Walking in Honesty, Truth and Integrity.*

Now in his 43rd year as a minister of the gospel of Christ and teacher of God's Word, Kenneth is the recording artist of such award-winning albums as his Grammy-nominated *Only the Redeemed, In His Presence, He Is Jehovah, Just a Closer Walk* and his most recently released *Big Band Gospel* album. He also co-stars as the character Wichita Slim in the children's adventure videos *The Gunslinger, Covenant Rider* and the movie *The Treasure of Eagle Mountain,* and as Daniel Lyon in the *Commander Kellie and the Superkids*_{SM} videos *Armor of Light* and *Judgment: The Trial of Commander Kellie.*

With the help of offices and staff in the United States, Canada, England, Australia, South Africa and Ukraine, Kenneth is fulfilling his vision to boldly preach the uncompromised Word of God from the top of this world, to the bottom, and all the way around. His ministry reaches millions of people worldwide through daily and Sunday TV broadcasts, magazines, teaching audios and videos, conventions and campaigns, and the World Wide Web.

Learn more about Kenneth Copeland Ministries by visiting our Web site at **www.kcm.org**

Books Available From
Kenneth Copeland Ministries

by Kenneth Copeland

* A Ceremony of Marriage
  A Matter of Choice
  Blessed to Be a Blessing
  Covenant of Blood
  Faith and Patience—The Power Twins
* Freedom From Fear
  Giving and Receiving
  Honor—Walking in Honesty, Truth and Integrity
  How to Conquer Strife
  How to Discipline Your Flesh
  How to Receive Communion
  In Love There Is No Fear
  Know Your Enemy
  Living at the End of Time—A Time of
     Supernatural Increase
  Love Letters From Heaven
  Love Never Fails
* Mercy—The Divine Rescue of the Human Race
* Now Are We in Christ Jesus
  One Nation Under God (gift book with CD enclosed)
* Our Covenant With God
  Partnership—Sharing the Vision, Sharing the Grace
* Prayer—Your Foundation for Success
* Prosperity: The Choice Is Yours
  Rumors of War
* Sensitivity of Heart
* Six Steps to Excellence in Ministry
* Sorrow Not! Winning Over Grief and Sorrow
* The Decision Is Yours

by Gloria Copeland

Hidden Treasures

Live Long, Finish Strong

Living in Heaven's Blessings Now

Looking for a Receiver

* Love—The Secret to Your Success

No Deposit—No Return

Pleasing the Father

Pressing In—It's Worth It All

Shine On!

The Grace That Makes Us Holy

The Power to Live a New Life

The Protection of Angels

There Is No High Like the Most High

The Secret Place of God's Protection (gift book with CD enclosed)

The Unbeatable Spirit of Faith

This Same Jesus

To Know Him

True Prosperity

Walk With God

Well Worth the Wait

Words That Heal (gift book with CD enclosed)

Your Promise of Protection—The Power of the 91st Psalm

Books Co-Authored by Kenneth and Gloria Copeland

Family Promises

Healing Promises

Prosperity Promises

Protection Promises

* From Faith to Faith—A Daily Guide to Victory

From Faith to Faith—A Perpetual Calendar

He Did It All for You

Lifeline Series: Practical Tools for Everyday Needs
- Healing & Wellness: Your 10-Day Spiritual Action Plan
- Your 10-Day Spiritual Action Plan for Complete
  Financial Breakthrough
- Your 10-Day Spiritual Action Plan for Building
  Relationships That Last

One Word From God Can Change Your Life

One Word From God Series:
- One Word From God Can Change Your Destiny
- One Word From God Can Change Your Family
- One Word From God Can Change Your Finances
- One Word From God Can Change Your Formula
  for Success
- One Word From God Can Change Your Health
- One Word From God Can Change Your Nation
- One Word From God Can Change Your Prayer Life
- One Word From God Can Change
  Your Relationships

Load Up—A Youth Devotional
Over the Edge—A Youth Devotional
Pursuit of His Presence—A Daily Devotional
Pursuit of His Presence—A Perpetual Calendar
Raising Children Without Fear

Other Books Published by KCP

Hello. My Name Is God. by Jeremy Pearsons
John G. Lake—His Life, His Sermons, His Boldness of Faith
Protecting Your Family in Dangerous Times
      by Kellie Copeland Swisher
The Holiest of All by Andrew Murray
The New Testament in Modern Speech
      by Richard Francis Weymouth

* Available in Spanish

The Rabbi From Burbank by Isidor Zwirn and Bob Owen
Unchained! by Mac Gober

Products Designed for Today's Children and Youth

And Jesus Healed Them All (confession book and
  CD gift package)
Baby Praise Board Book
Baby Praise Christmas Board Book
Noah's Ark Coloring Book
The Best of *Shout!* Adventure Comics
The *Shout!* Giant Flip Coloring Book
The *Shout!* Joke Book
The *Shout!* Super-Activity Book
Wichita Slim's Campfire Stories

*Commander Kellie and the Superkids*_{SM} Books:

Superkid Academy Children's Church Curriculum
  (DVD/CD curriculum)
• Volume 1—My Father Loves Me!
• Volume 2—The Fruit of the Spirit in You
• Volume 3—The Sweet Life
• Volume 4—Living in THE BLESSING

The SWORD Adventure Book
*Commander Kellie and the Superkids*_{SM}
  Solve-It-Yourself Mysteries
*Commander Kellie and the Superkids*_{SM} Adventure Series:
  Middle Grade Novels by Christopher P.N. Maselli:

  #1 The Mysterious Presence
  #2 The Quest for the Second Half
  #3 Escape From Jungle Island
  #4 In Pursuit of the Enemy
  #5 Caged Rivalry

World Offices
Kenneth Copeland Ministries

For more information about KCM and our products,
please write to the office nearest you:

Kenneth Copeland Ministries
Fort Worth, TX 76192-0001

Kenneth Copeland
Locked Bag 2600
Mansfield Delivery Centre
QUEENSLAND 4122
AUSTRALIA

Kenneth Copeland
Post Office Box 15
BATH
BA1 3XN
U.K.

Kenneth Copeland
Private Bag X 909
FONTAINEBLEAU
2032
REPUBLIC OF
SOUTH AFRICA

Kenneth Copeland
PO Box 3111 STN LCD 1
Langley BC V3A 4R3
CANADA

Kenneth Copeland Ministries
Post Office Box 84
L'VIV 79000
UKRAINE

We're Here for You!

Believer's Voice of Victory Television Broadcast

Join Kenneth and Gloria Copeland and the *Believer's Voice of Victory* broadcasts Monday through Friday and on Sunday each week, and learn how faith in God's Word can take your life from ordinary to extraordinary. This teaching from God's Word is designed to get you where you want to be—*on top!*

You can catch the *Believer's Voice of Victory* broadcast on your local, cable or satellite channels.* Also available 24 hours on webcast at BVOV.TV.

*Check your local listings for times and stations in your area.

Believer's Voice of Victory Magazine

Enjoy inspired teaching and encouragement from Kenneth and Gloria Copeland and guest ministers each month in the *Believer's Voice of Victory* magazine. Also included are real-life testimonies of God's miraculous power and divine intervention in the lives of people just like you!

It's more than just a magazine—it's a ministry.

To receive a FREE subscription to
Believer's Voice of Victory, write to:

Kenneth Copeland Ministries
Fort Worth, TX 76192-0001
Or call:
800-600-7395
(7 a.m.-5 p.m. CT)
Or visit our Web site at:
www.kcm.org

If you are writing from outside the U.S., please contact the
KCM office nearest you. Addresses for all Kenneth Copeland
Ministries offices are listed on the previous pages.